Instant New iPad Features in iOS 6 How-to

Learn to use Mail, iCloud, Photo Stream, iPhoto, iWorks, iTunes, iMovie, and Garageband through easy-to-follow recipes

Renee J. Valdez

BIRMINGHAM - MUMBAI

Instant New iPad Features in iOS 6 How-to

First published: January 2013

Production Reference: 1210113

Published by Packt Publishing Ltd.
Livery Place
35 Livery Street
Birmingham B3 2PB, UK.

ISBN 978-1-78216-046-5

www.packtpub.com

Credits

Author
Renee J. Valdez

Reviewers
Allen Sherrod

Jayant C. Varma

Acquisition Editor
Usha Iyer

Commissioning Editor
Meeta Rajani

Technical Editor
Dennis John

Copy Editor
Brandt D'Mello

Project Coordinator
Esha Thakker

Proofreader
Maria Gould

Graphics
Aparna Bhagat

Production Coordinator
Aparna Bhagat

Cover Work
Aparna Bhagat

Cover Image
Manu Joseph

About the Author

Renee J. Valdez has been working in the tech industry for over 6 years. Focusing on mobile and tablet media, she is involved in content delivery and the production of applications across multiple platforms.

When she's not tinkering with the latest device, she enjoys punk rock, cats, and traveling.

I'd like to thank my friends and family for encouraging me throughout the writing process. A big thank you to the editors and staff behind the book. Your patience was appreciated.

About the Reviewers

Allen Sherrod is currently a senior iOS developer of interactive apps with several apps in the iTunes store, including an app for the upcoming DreamWorks movie *Rise of the Guardians*. He started with programming in high school as he learned OpenGL and Direct3D for the first time. From there, he took to game development as a hobby while in college, wrote several books on it, and now currently creates interactive storybook and comic apps for mobile platforms. He has also authored and co-authored several books on gaming, such as *Essential XNA Game Studio 2.0 Programming*, *Data Structures and Algorithms for Game Developers*, and *Beginning DirectX 11 Game Programming*, to name a few.

> I would like to thank my family and friends for always supporting and helping me over the years.

Jayant C. Varma has been a veteran for over 20 years in the world of technology. He has vast and rich experience spanning across several countries and industries (managing IT operations). Over these years, he has worked across a wide range of systems and languages, both computer and human. Starting off with what was fun and games with Basic and Z80 on the ZX Spectrum, he has now come full circle, back to games and apps on mobile devices. He has been with mobile development from the early 2000s when Microsoft released the PocketPC Mobile OS based on Windows CE. Currently, he is based in Australia and has founded OZApps (http://www.oz-apps.com), a one-stop shop consultancy for companies wanting to implement and enhance their mobile strategy. He has seen both sides of the industry from a commercial aspect as an IT manager for the automobile sector (BMW and Nissan), and from an academic perspective with teaching young graduates and conducting training and running workshops on mobile development at the University.

He is the author of *Learn Lua for iOS Game Development*, *Apress* (http://www.apress.com/9781430246626). He also helps developers through his blog at http://howto.oz-apps.com and a review site at http://reviewme.oz-apps.com. You can also follow him on Twitter; his Twitter handles are @ozapps, @whatsin4me, and @learnlua.

www.packtpub.com

Support files, eBooks, discount offers and more

You might want to visit www.packtpub.com for support files and downloads related to your book.

Did you know that Packt offers eBook versions of every book published, with PDF and ePub files available? You can upgrade to the eBook version at www.packtpub.com and as a print book customer, you are entitled to a discount on the eBook copy. Get in touch with us at service@packtpub.com for more details.

At www.packtpub.com, you can also read a collection of free technical articles, sign up for a range of free newsletters and receive exclusive discounts and offers on Packt books and eBooks.

http://packtlib.packtpub.com

Do you need instant solutions to your IT questions? PacktLib is Packt's online digital book library. Here, you can access, read and search across Packt's entire library of books.

Why Subscribe?

- ▸ Fully searchable across every book published by Packt
- ▸ Copy and paste, print, and bookmark content
- ▸ On demand and accessible via web browser

Free Access for Packt account holders

If you have an account with Packt at www.packtpub.com, you can use this to access PacktLib today and view nine entirely free books. Simply use your login credentials for immediate access.

Table of Contents

Preface

Apple's iPad has revolutionized the way we consume and edit content. This has resulted in a major shift that many are now starting to adopt. The new iPad's display and processing power allow for a rich media experience that is unlike any other. Instead of solely consuming media, you can create, edit, and manage everything from Excel documents to HD home movies. The multi-touch interface makes creating and editing intuitive. iCloud syncs documents, movies, music, and images to the cloud for access from all of your Apple devices. By exploring Apple's suite of apps designed specially for the iPad, these recipes provide easy-to-follow steps enabling you to become a power user.

What this book covers

New iPad features and native applications (Must know): This recipe offers a break down of the apps that come natively installed on the new iPad. We'll briefly introduce each application we'll be working with in the book.

Working with the Mail application (Must know): This recipe is a walkthrough of the e-mail set up process. We'll also learn about Mail's VIP feature.

Adding an @iCloud.com e-mail address (Should know): This recipe covers details about iCloud and its workings. Want to know what the cloud is and what we're able to sync to the cloud? This recipe will answer your questions and guide you through the process of setting up your iPad for iCloud syncing.

Photos – editing, sharing, and Photo Stream (Should know): This recipe gets into the details of editing images and sharing them between devices. We'll edit an image and go over the editing capabilities of the Photos app. With Photo Stream, we'll learn what it's all about and why it's such a cool feature.

iPhoto – editing, sharing, and importing (Should know): This recipe gives more detailed information about photo editing, delving into iPhoto and its many features. We'll learn basic editing skills but will work with different tools that are more robust than what's offered in the Photos application.

iMovie – capturing, editing, and sharing your footage (Should know): This recipe will open the curtain to iMovie, giving a high-level overview of what it has to offer. We'll play with some footage and learn how to share our projects.

iWork – Keynote, Numbers, and Pages (Must know): This recipe explains each of the applications in the iWork suite. Similar to Microsoft's PowerPoint, Excel, and Word, the apps in iWork make creating and editing easy. Presentations, spreadsheets, and documents are all explored in this recipe.

Starting a Keynote presentation (Should know): This recipe gets us through a brief but complete presentation. Each step increases our knowledge of the user interface, making the upcoming sections in the iWork applications suite more familiar.

Numbers – starting and editing a spreadsheet (Must know): This recipe works through a template, using frequently used actions in spreadsheets such as those created in Excel.

Pages – starting and editing a document (Should know): This recipe teaches us how to create a typical word document. We'll look at templates and go through some basic editing skills.

Sharing and syncing documents from Keynote, Numbers, and Pages (Should know): This recipe shows us how to share documents across each of the iWork applications. This can also be considered an in-depth look at sharing. A lot of the conventions carry over into other applications.

iBooks – downloading from iBookstore and importing PDFs (Should know): This recipe starts with downloading books from the store and then goes into importing PDFs into our library. Apart from reading books, being able to read PDF-based documents is a useful tool to learn.

Garageband – a basic project (Become an expert): This recipe will showcase the iPad's ability to create and edit music. In this recipe, we'll create a project and learn about Garageband's many features.

What you need for this book

You will need an iPad running iOS 6. It's also good to take some images and videos using the Camera application so you have media to work with. It's as easy as opening the Camera app and hitting the circular button with the red dot in the middle.

Who this book is for

This book is for anyone who is somewhat familiar with the iPad but wants to get an overview of its new features. A basic understanding of touch devices is good, but not necessary. The recipes walk you through everything you need to know to accomplish each task. Good for both the novice and the expert, there's something in here for everyone.

Conventions

In this book, you will find a number of styles of text that distinguish between different kinds of information. Here are some examples of these styles, and an explanation of their meaning.

New terms and **important words** are shown in bold. Words that you see on the screen, in menus or dialog boxes for example, appear in the text like this: "After selecting **Gmail** we're taken to a screen with fields for **Name**, **Email**, **Password**, and **Description**".

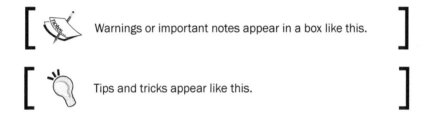

Warnings or important notes appear in a box like this.

Tips and tricks appear like this.

Reader feedback

Feedback from our readers is always welcome. Let us know what you think about this book— what you liked or may have disliked. Reader feedback is important for us to develop titles that you really get the most out of.

To send us general feedback, simply send an e-mail to feedback@packtpub.com, and mention the book title via the subject of your message.

If there is a book that you need and would like to see us publish, please send us a note in the **SUGGEST A TITLE** form on www.packtpub.com or e-mail suggest@packtpub.com.

If there is a topic that you have expertise in and you are interested in either writing or contributing to a book, see our author guide on www.packtpub.com/authors.

Customer support

Now that you are the proud owner of a Packt book, we have a number of things to help you to get the most from your purchase.

Errata

Although we have taken every care to ensure the accuracy of our content, mistakes do happen. If you find a mistake in one of our books—maybe a mistake in the text or the code—we would be grateful if you would report this to us. By doing so, you can save other readers from frustration and help us improve subsequent versions of this book. If you find any errata, please report them by visiting `http://www.packtpub.com/support`, selecting your book, clicking on the **errata submission form** link, and entering the details of your errata. Once your errata are verified, your submission will be accepted and the errata will be uploaded on our website, or added to any list of existing errata, under the Errata section of that title. Any existing errata can be viewed by selecting your title from `http://www.packtpub.com/support`.

Piracy

Piracy of copyright material on the Internet is an ongoing problem across all media. At Packt, we take the protection of our copyright and licenses very seriously. If you come across any illegal copies of our works, in any form, on the Internet, please provide us with the location address or website name immediately so that we can pursue a remedy.

Please contact us at `copyright@packtpub.com` with a link to the suspected pirated material.

We appreciate your help in protecting our authors, and our ability to bring you valuable content.

Questions

You can contact us at `questions@packtpub.com` if you are having a problem with any aspect of the book, and we will do our best to address it.

Instant New iPad Features in iOS 6 How-to

The new iPad, released in March 2012, took the iPad 2 and gave it a Retina display, twice the screen resolution, a dual-core processor, and 4G LTE wireless data capability. In addition, the new iPad is lighter and thinner than its predecessor. Comparing it with the iPad 2, these upgrades equate to a richer, more beautiful display, faster processing, and access to a faster data network in a thinner, lighter package.

But what makes an iPad an iPad? Its apps! This tablet comes with 21 built-in applications, designed specifically for the device. Now, with iOS 6, these applications have improved and come with more features and better integration with the operating system.

In the following recipes we'll explore some of the applications that illustrate the new iPad's features. Some of these applications are native to the device, and others are premium, available in the App Store.

New iPad features and native applications (Must know)

We're going to identify some of the applications that come built-in to the new iPad. The applications designed by Apple for the iPad are Safari, Mail, Photos, FaceTime, Maps, Siri, Newsstand, Messages, Calendar, Reminders, Contacts, App Store, iTunes, Music, Videos, Notes, Camera, Photo Booth, Clock, Game Center, and Settings.

Let's get started by exploring these applications.

Getting ready

▶ Locate the Mail, Photos, App Store, iTunes, Music, and Settings apps

▶ For details on each app, visit `http://www.apple.com/ipad/built-in-apps/`

How to do it...

These apps form the base of the iPad and by themselves can satisfy most of our media and communication needs. We'll delve deeper into each of the following apps in the upcoming recipes.

▶ Mail

▶ Photos

▶ App Store

▶ iTunes and Music

▶ Settings

How it works...

The applications can work together to provide a unifying experience. From the Photos app, we are able to share photos via the Mail application. Purchasing music in iTunes will allow us playback in our Music app. Ubiquity is what makes this device and its apps so useful.

There's more...

In the next recipe, we'll dig deeper into Mail, setting up accounts, and getting the new features enabled.

Working with the Mail application (Must know)

The Mail application could be one of the most-used applications on iPad. It's full of customizable features and makes handling multiple e-mail addresses a breeze. Many of us have at least two e-mail addresses, work and personal. Let's set up our mailbox.

Getting ready

You must have an e-mail address to proceed.

How to do it...

1. Open up the **Settings** application and select **Mail, Contacts, Calendars** from the left-hand menu, as shown in the following screenshot:

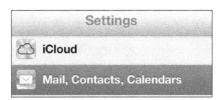

2. To the right, we see **Accounts**. Select **Add Account...**, as shown in the following screenshot:

3. We're taken to a menu with a variety of options as shown:

4. For this example, we're going to select **Gmail**. Setting up other e-mail addresses is very similar and requires the same information. The exceptions are setting up **iCloud**, **Exchange**, or **Other** accounts. The task of setting these up is a bit more advanced.

5. Let's set it up for a Gmail address. After selecting **Gmail**, we're taken to a screen with the fields **Name**, **Email**, **Password**, and **Description**, as shown in the following screenshot:

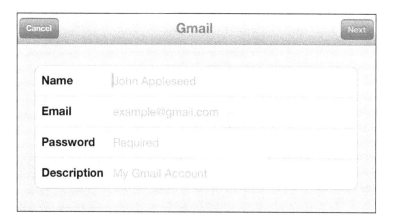

6. We'll enter our name as we'd like it to appear in our outgoing messages. Then, we'll enter our e-mail address, password, and a description of the account. Hitting **Next** will finish up the process, verifying the e-mail address.

7. When complete, we're given the options of turning this address **ON** or **OFF**. Keeping it **ON** will allow our e-mail messages to appear on the iPad. We definitely want this e-mail address **ON**; whether or not we decide to enable calendars and notes isn't relevant to this task. Having either turned on will sync our **Calendar** and **Notes** data associated with this e-mail address. Tap **Save**:

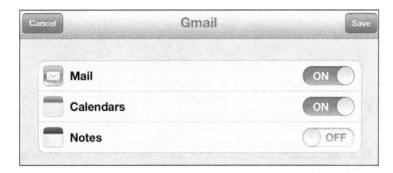

8. Now that we've got an e-mail address, let's set up a VIP inbox. New in iOS 6, this filtered inbox is a mix of contacts from all of our e-mail addresses allowing us to create a special inbox with contacts we deem important. This ensures that they don't get overlooked when going from device to device and e-mail address to e-mail address.

How it works...

The **Mail** app organizes multiple e-mail addresses, e-mail threads, and adds the feature of a **VIP** inbox for our most important contacts. The setup is fairly simple.

We begin by tapping **Add VIP...**, as shown in the following screenshot:

This brings up all of our contacts associated with our e-mail address. Selecting a contact adds them to the **VIP List**, as shown in the following screenshot:

There's more...

Within the settings for **Mail**, we saw **iCloud** as an optional e-mail account. Setting up an iCloud e-mail address is important for all of our future iCloud usage. **iTunes**, **iBooks**, **App Store**, and other apps where content can be auto-synced to iCloud all require an iCloud e-mail address that's tied to one master **Apple ID**.

In the following recipe, we'll learn all about iCloud and will set up our very own iCloud e-mail address.

Adding an @iCloud.com e-mail address (Should know)

iCloud is an all-encompassing term for Apple's **SyncServices**. Meant to keep files ubiquitous across all Apple devices, the service acts as a backup, leaving our files in the cloud where we'll have access to them on our iPhone, iPod Touch, or Mac. We can also access our files via www.iCloud.com.

Why enable this? Aside from the anytime, anywhere access, the backup feature is one that should not be overlooked. We may not need to access our documents or photos from everywhere, but having a backup of our contacts, photos, calendars, and documents is pretty great, especially when it happens automatically.

We'll begin by setting up iCloud on our iPad.

Getting ready

An Apple ID is required in order to proceed. You most likely already have an Apple ID, but if not, you can get one from the setup screen, as shown in the following steps.

How to do it...

1. From the **Settings** app in **Mail, Contacts, Calendars**, select **Add Account...**, and then select **iCloud**.

2. We're prompted to enter an Apple ID and password. If you don't have one, tap **Get a Free Apple ID** and follow the ensuing steps:

3. Enter your Apple ID and password, and then tap **Next**. The following screen appears, and we're prompted to turn on or off various iCloud sync features. Turn them all on, including **Photo Stream** (which does not default to **ON**, so double check that it's enabled):

4. Tap **Save** and we're done. We've got iCloud enabled! We were also automatically given an iCloud e-mail address. We now see our account listed in the **Accounts** list view, as shown in the following screenshot:

5. Now tap **iCloud** to view all of our settings one more time. Scroll to the bottom of the list and select **Storage & Backup**, as shown in the following screenshot:

6. Now we need to make a decision. Do we want to enable **iCloud Backup**? Enabling this will avoid the need to manually back up our iPad using the cable, our computer, and iTunes. iCloud allows us to do this when our iPad is locked and connected to Wi-Fi. Flip the switch to **ON**; we're given a prompt alerting us to the changes we've just made, as shown in the following screenshot. This is telling us that when we plug our iPad into our computer, it will not sync automatically. This is because it will have been syncing via **iCloud Backup** and there is no need for the sync when you plug in your device. Everything will already be backed up, up to 5 GB.

How it works...

We are setting up the foundation of iCloud, enabling it in mail and using **iCloud Backup** to sync our Contacts, Camera Roll, Calendars, and Documents & Data apps.

In the next recipe, we'll go into the **Photos** app, looking at **Photo Stream**. We'll also cover the editing powers of **iPhoto**, a premium app used for editing images captured on the iPad, iPhone, or iPod Touch.

Photos – editing, sharing, and Photo Stream (Should know)

The **Photos** app is native to the iPad and is a great way to organize, sync, and share your photos. We'll begin by exploring the interface and then dig a little deeper into editing, sharing, and Photo Stream.

Getting ready

Let's make sure we have a few photos in **Camera Roll**. If you don't have any photos, take a couple of pictures with the iPad, using the **Camera** app.

How to do it...

1. Open the **Photos** app and tap on a photo. In the upper-right corner, we see the **Edit**, **Slideshow**, and the share icons.

2. Tap **Edit** and the edit menu is displayed at the bottom of the screen, as shown in the following screenshot:

   - Selecting **Rotate** will rotate your photo in counter-clockwise, 90-degree rotations.
   - **Enhance** will adjust the lighting of the photo automatically. There are no added options for more control of the enhancements. It's a one-tap fix.

❏ **Red-Eye** will correct red-eye with a simple tap on the eye. At the bottom of the screen, the following message appears:

Tap each red-eye. Tap again to undo.

❏ Tapping **Crop** brings up a grid that is scaled by touching the corners or any of the lines encompassing the gridded area. We can move the image around, behind the grid, by touching the image and sliding it around.

3. Tap **Crop** to begin editing an image.

4. Note that a new menu appears at the bottom of the screen. We see **Constrain** and **Reset**, as shown in the following screenshot. **Constrain** will crop the image to a common set of dimensions, and **Reset** brings the entire image back into the grid.

5. Tap **Crop** in the upper-right corner of the screen, and the menu will change, as shown in the following screenshot. Tap **Save**, and we will have successfully edited a photo.

6. Now that we've successfully edited a photo, let's share it with **Photo Stream**. What is **Photo Stream**? It's a section in the cloud where we are able to save photos and access them from other Apple devices.

   To share, tap on the share icon. A menu pops up with a variety of options. We'll be selecting **Photo Stream**, as shown in the following screenshot:

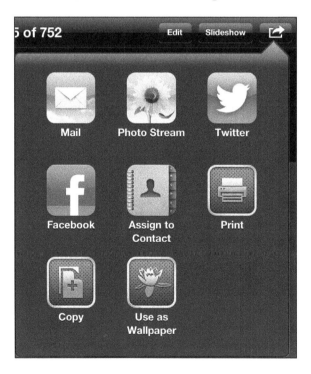

7. Sharing to **Photo Stream** brings up our options. You'll notice a **To:** field. This will share to an e-mail address, something we won't be doing in this exercise. We'll be creating a **Photo Stream** folder called **My Edits**, as shown in the following screenshot:

8. Tapping **Next** will allow for a comment and the ability to finalize your share by hitting **Post**. Your photo is now in the cloud and available in the **Photo Stream** tab, in the **Photos** app, shown in the following screenshot:

Photo Stream images will be available on other iCloud-enabled devices such as the iPhone, iPod Touch, or Apple TV.

In the following recipe we'll take our photo editing skills a bit further by exploring iPhoto.

iPhoto – editing, sharing, and importing (Should know)

Part of Apple's iLife suite, iPhoto, is a premium app selling for $4.99 in the App Store. With multi-touch gestures, you can edit photos using a huge variety of tools. As part of the Apple suite, the app is compatible with iCloud, making your photos editable from any device that has iPhoto installed, including your computer.

In the previous recipe on the native **Photos** app, we covered basic photo editing such as rotating, cropping, enhancing, and red-eye removal. In iPhoto we've got so much more. Now we'll explore some of the gestures and some advanced features.

Getting ready

In order to continue the following set of instructions, you must download iPhoto for $4.99 from the App Store.

We already have some photos in the **Camera Roll** app from the previous recipe, and those are fine to use for this exercise in exploration.

How to do it...

There's a lot going on in this app, and we could easily devote an entire book to it. Let's cover some of the basics of the interface first. Then we'll use some of those tools.

1. Open the app and tap the **Camera Roll** album shown in the following screenshot:

2. Tapping **Camera Roll** will open up the folder and give us a slew of editing options. Take some time to look at all of the icons appearing in the upper and lower portion of the screen. Focus on the tools in the upper-left corner and tap the question mark icon. Tapping that icon will reveal a description of all the tools appearing on the page. The following screenshot shows the upper menu with descriptions:

3. Take a look at the options on the lower menu, shown in the following screenshot. Some of the options are familiar, based on our use of the **Photos** app. **Crop & Straighten**, **Auto-Enhance**, and **Rotate** are here, but you'll notice that they're more refined and provide more options. This lower menu is where all of the magic happens.

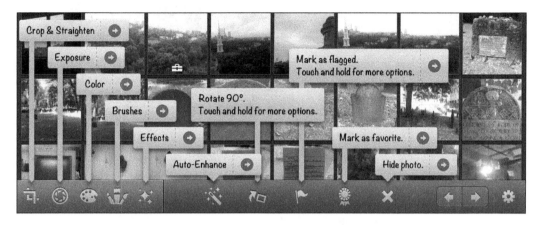

- **Crop & Straighten** allows us to straighten out images using gestures and a guide. **Rotate** offers us more, allowing us to rotate the image in increments using a two-finger twist gesture or the rotator at the bottom of screen, as shown in the following screenshot:

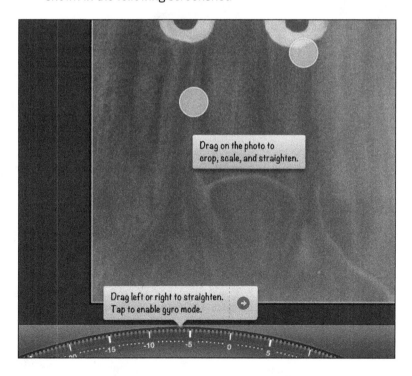

❑ **Exposure** and **Color** are pretty detailed and can make our reds redder and blues bluer. If we want to enhance a photo, these are the best tools do to so. You can see what these options are capable of by tapping on areas of the photo and adjusting the sliders, as shown in the following screenshot:

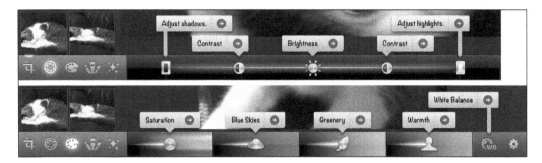

❑ **Brushes** offers many options from color correction to sharpening an image. **Effects** are fun extras to make your photos unique. Both are shown in the following screenshot:

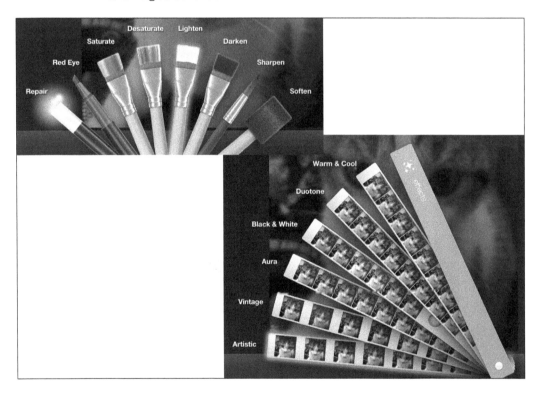

4. Let's select an effect for our photo. Tap **Black & White**. Now we see even more options appear in the lower menu. This will help us refine the effect. Tap one of the options shown in the following screenshot. The option farthest to the right in the following screenshot will bring up the menu of effects again. Give it a try.

5. Now that we've applied the **Black & White** effect to our photo, let's save it by using the share icon in the upper-right corner, as shown in the following screenshot:

6. Here we see many different options. To save this photo to our iPad, we'd tap **Camera Roll** and choose the selected image.

    ❑ Sharing to iTunes is a quick tap, and the image will be available in iTunes when we plug our iPad in to the computer

❑ **Journal** is an extra feature in iPhoto that allows you create photo journals using a variety of templates

❑ Sharing via social media such as Twitter, Flickr, and Facebook is intuitive and never more than a few taps away

7. Let's focus on the **Beam** option. Beaming allows us to send a photo to another iOS device. To do this, both devices must be on the same wireless network and must be running iPhoto. Once you tap **Beam** and select the photo, iPhoto will begin searching for devices in range, as shown in the following screenshot:

How it works...

iPhoto is a hefty application. Aside from the well-designed interface and editing capabilities, its strongest feature is the ubiquity it offers when using multiple Apple products. It saves us from being tethered to our computers while managing and editing our photos.

There's more...

In the next recipe we'll explore another app from Apple's iLife suite, iMovie.

Importing photos into iPhoto

If we've got **Photo Stream** enabled on our iPhone and iPod Touch, the act of importing is moot. Any photo taken on devices with **Photo Stream** enabled will automatically sync those photos to iCloud, making them available on our new iPad and in iPhoto on our computers.

Suppose that we have photos on a non-Apple digital camera that we want to import into iPhoto on our iPad. For this, our best option is to plug our digital camera into our computer and import the images into iPhoto. If we don't have iPhoto on our computer, we can purchase an iPad Camera Connection Kit, and that will get the job done for us.

iMovie – capturing, editing, and sharing your footage (Should know)

iMovie is another application in Apple's iLife suite. It's $4.99 in the App Store and offers multi-touch editing capabilities and lots of share options. In this recipe we'll learn some of its basic features and familiarize ourselves with the common iconography.

Getting ready

In order to continue and follow the instructions in this section, you must download iMovie from the app store. Remember, it's a premium app for $4.99.

How to do it...

1. To start a new project, tap the plus icon. This brings up a menu where we can select **New Project** or **New Trailer**, as shown in the following screenshot:

❑ **New Trailer** creates a short video trailer using pre-made templates and sets it up in the manner of a storyboard. We can use video from the **Camera Roll** app, photos stored on our iPad, and music stored in the Music app.

❑ Like iPhoto, iMovie has a lot of features, so we're going to be focusing on **New Project**. A project allows us to make a movie of any length, using the same sources, video, music, and photos. We also have a variety of templates we can use.

2. Tap on **New Project**. We're taken to the editing interface with a media browser, timeline, and a video viewer.

❑ The media browser shows us the available media on our iPad. The following screenshot shows the **Video** tab in the media browser. Sliding your finger within a video will preview it in the video viewer. Double-tapping a video will bring the video into the timeline:

❏ The video icon to the left displays all of the video in our **Camera Roll** app. The photos icon (shown by two overlapping boxes) in the middle displays the photos located in our **Camera Roll** app, and the music note icon brings up the music located in our Music app, as shown in the following screenshot:

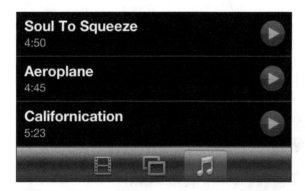

3. If no video exists on our iPad, we're able to shoot video directly into the app, using the video camera icon located on the right, just below the video viewer. Once the icon is tapped, our screen goes into record mode. To record some video, simply tap on the record button (the one with a red dot). Let's record some video of our surroundings and use that video to explore the editing interface. Tap on the record button, and when finished, tap again. Then, tap on the **Use** button in the lower-right corner (shown in the following screenshot):

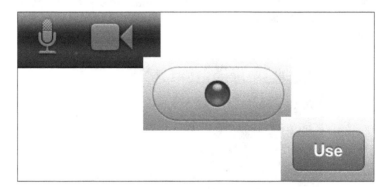

4. This brings our video into our project. You can see our video in the video viewer, timeline, and media browser. Editing the clip length is done by tapping on either side of the video and sliding it to the desired length. When selected, the video is highlighted and we can double-tap it to display the clip settings, as shown in the following screenshot:

5. Here we see **Title Style**, **Location**, an audio icon, and a **Delete Clip** button. We can set the title of the clip, the location, and can adjust its audio. Let's go ahead and select **Title Style** and type in a title for our video clip.

6. What determines where our title appears? Our project settings, located in the upper-right hand side menu, determine the look and feel of our project. There's a selection of templates in the upper row. Below that, we see **Theme Music**, **Loop Background Music**, **Fade in from black**, and **Fade out to black**, as shown in the following screenshot:

7. Flip both fades to **ON** and tap outside of the menu. Then play the clip back using the play button. Note that the color changes to black at the beginning and end of the clip.

8. Try out some of the templates to explore the look and feel of each one.

9. To view the audio settings of our video clip, tap on the audio icon and then double-tap on the video in the timeline, as shown in the following screenshot:

10. Go ahead and use some media from the browser mentioned in steps 2 and 3, and select some media by double-tapping on **Photos** and **Music**. We want to have something to export, so play around for a bit.

11. If at any point you want to undo something, there's a handy **Undo** button in the upper-right corner of the screen. Also located in the upper menu above the video viewer is the iMovie Projects icon. Both the **Undo** and iMovie Projects icons can be seen in the following screenshot:

12. Let's tap on that iMovie Projects icon so we can get back to the main menu for iMovie. Here our project is selected. When we have more than one project; they will all display in a row in this view. In the lower menu, we see the plus, play, share, Copy from iTunes, and the trashcan icons, as shown in the following screenshot:

❑ We used the plus icon when we started the project, and the play icon plays back our project. The Copy from iTunes icon will copy projects you have synced using iTunes, something that's a bit more advanced and involves the use of multiple devices editing the same project. The trashcan icon deletes your project.

13. Let's focus on the share icon. Tap on the share icon to view all of our share options, as shown in the following screenshot:

14. We can share movies to our **Camera Roll** and a variety of social media sites. We can also send our project to iTunes. This will allow us access to the project when we connect our device to **iTunes**. When our iPad is plugged in to our computer, we see our projects at the bottom of the **Apps** menu, as shown in the following screenshot:

How it works...

iMovie utilizes the processing power of the iPad while using all of the media on our iPad. It allows us to create trailers and movie projects using a touch interface that is easy to grasp. There's a lot to this app and we've just scratched the surface, but being familiar with the menu options gets us a long way.

There's more...

Now that we've explored the apps in Apple's iLife suite, let's get into the apps in the iWorks suite. In the following recipes, we'll learn all about Apple's Pages, Numbers, and Keynote apps.

Importing video into iMovie

This is no easy task. One method is purchasing a Camera Connection Kit. This allows us to plug a device directly into our iPad where images and video can be imported. Another method is e-mailing video files. This isn't always useful as we're limited by file size, and video files are quite large. The last option requires a few steps. We'd need to plug in our device with the video into our computer and import it using iPhoto. Then we'd plug our iPad into our computer and sync the contents to iPhoto.

Apple's iWork suite offers portable productivity synced across all of your devices, including your computer. Keynote, Numbers, and Pages, the apps that make up the iWork suite, do not come native in the new iPad, but if you're looking for an easy way to create, edit, and store your documents, this is the way to go.

Typically purchased as the whole suite, the option of purchasing individually is available in the App Store. Each app goes for $4.99.

iWork – Keynote, Numbers, and Pages (Must know)

What are these applications and why are they useful? Well, we're accustomed to creating and editing our documents on a computer, usually in Word, Excel, and PowerPoint. This is changing and we're now spending more time on our portable devices than at our actual computers. The most important thing when charting these waters is compatibility. We'll learn more about the compatibility of these apps with commonly used file types in the following exercise.

Getting ready

To proceed with the ensuing set of instructions, you must download each of the following applications from the App Store.

- Download **Keynote**, a presentation app that is capable of creating, editing, reading, and exporting a number of popular file formats. Keynote utilizes the iPad's large screen with familiar multi-touch gestures that make it intuitive and fast. You can edit and review on the go, with each presentation auto-syncing to Keynote in iCloud.

- Download **Numbers**, an app that brings touch to spreadsheets. It's quick and makes it easy to create impressive data displays using tables, charts, and graphs. Since it's capable of editing, reading, and exporting common file types, compatibility outside of the suite is remarkably good. It syncs with iCloud, and you're able to view files on, and export them to, all of your devices.

- Download **Pages**, a word processor capable of reading Word documents as well as `.pdf` files. Editing is a breeze, and access is even easier as iCloud takes care of saving and backing up your documents. Exporting to `.doc` and `.pdf` ensures compatibility with other word-processing programs.

How to do it..

Open your **App Store** app and download each of the following applications:

1. **Keynote**
   - Create and edit presentations
   - Compatible with PowerPoint
   - Import and export `.ppt` and `.pptx`

2. **Numbers**

   ❑ Create and edit spreadsheets

   ❑ Compatible with Excel and Open Office

   ❑ Import and export `.xls`, `.xlsx`

3. **Pages**

   ❑ Create and edit documents

   ❑ Compatible with Word

   ❑ Import and export `.doc`, `.docx`

How it works...

Each app's files are attached to the Apple ID we made the purchase with. While logged in with that Apple ID on `www.iCloud.com`, the files will be synced and ready for download from any computer.

There's more...

If you have an iPhone, iPod Touch, or even another iPad, we can download Keynote, Numbers, and Pages using the same Apple ID at no cost. Having already purchased them for our iPad with our Apple ID, these applications are available to us on all of our devices sharing the same ID.

In the next recipe, we'll work with Keynote, the iOS equivalent of Excel. We'll create a simple presentation using Keynote's touch features and familiarize ourselves with the interface.

Downloading your application's counterpart

For application ubiquity, there's the option of downloading each of the application's counterpart for your OS X desktop or laptop. Each will cost you $19.99 and will sync along with all of your other devices. This is handy for those of us who still want the ability to edit on our computers.

Starting a Keynote presentation (Should know)

We'll start by exploring Keynote and creating a presentation using an image, text, data, and slide transitions.

Getting ready

Open up the **Keynote** app on your iPad. There aren't any presentations because we haven't created any yet, but we'll create a presentation now.

How to do it...

1. In the upper-left corner of the screen, there's a plus icon. Tapping the plus icon will prompt us to create a presentation. The plus symbol will be a running theme throughout the iWorks suite of apps. You'll notice it in later recipes on Numbers and Pages.

2. This then takes us to a selection of themes. You'll see a menu appear when you tap on the plus sign.

3. Let's select **Gradient** as it's a fairly common background for presentations. There are templates within each theme that help speed up common layouts. Tap the one titled **Gradient**. Then tap the plus icon in the lower-left corner and select the first slide. We'll begin by adding an image and title. Notice, in the following screenshot, that tapping the plus sign brings up the template's slides for that particular theme:

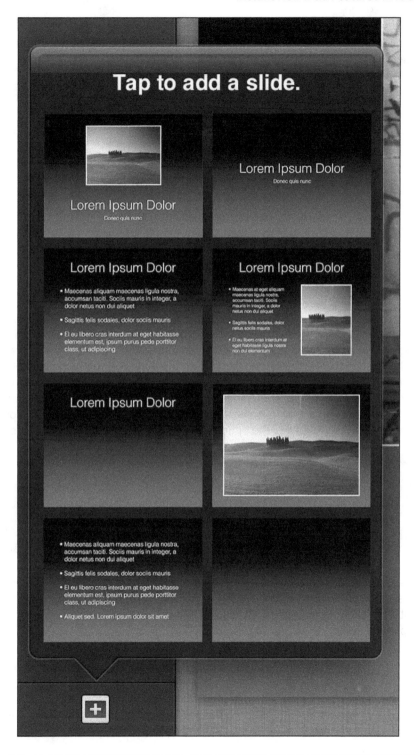

4. Editing the text is as easy as double-tapping, which will bring up the keyboard.

5. Tapping on the image icon on the bottom of the screen will give us the option of inserting an image from our library. Let's go ahead and tap the image icon so we can insert our own image.

6. Tap the image, and the editing options will appear. Take a moment to manipulate the image. Use pinch, twist, and swipe gestures and watch the image transform. Note the yellow guides that help align the image with the middle of the page and help align the selected object with other objects. We also have options for cutting, copying, deleting, and replacing the image. Animating is a bit more advanced. It's a feature that turns a static image into a moving object as the slide loads in and out. In the following screenshot, you'll see all of the options available when you have an object selected:

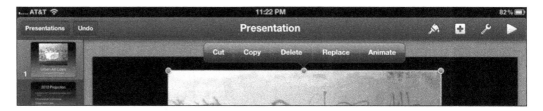

7. After manipulating the object, tap **Undo** in the upper-left corner of the screen. That's one of the many options sitting in the top menu. Take a moment to try them out. The following screenshot shows some of the options that drop down from the top menu items.

   ❑ **Presentations** takes us back to the main page of **Keynote**. You'll notice the presentation auto-save before it goes back to the app's home screen.

   ❑ **Undo** will revert any edit. Tap and hold to redo.

   ❑ The brush icon will format and style any object that is selected. The options will change depending on the object.

- The plus icon inserts objects into our presentations.
- The tool icon contains various tools to help you complete the presentation. This includes transitions and sharing options.
- The play button plays your presentation.

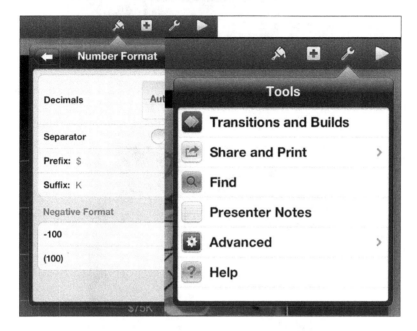

8. It's time to utilize these tools in order to complete our presentation. We've learned that tapping and using pinch and swipe gestures edits objects. We've inserted a new image, placed it on the page, and edited the text by simply tapping on the sample text and editing it.

9. Next, tap on the plus sign in the lower-left corner of the screen and add two more slides. Select the bulleted list and an empty slide so that we can customize it ourselves.

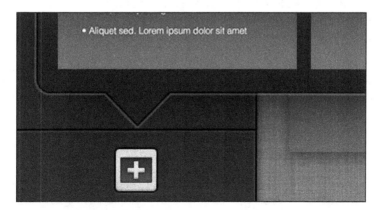

10. Each slide in the left-hand navigation window has a series of transition options. On tapping, select the plus icon sitting to the right-hand side of the word **None**. **None** indicates that no transition has been set, but if one were set, it'd be labeled here.

11. This pulls up a menu of transitions. Each slide can have a different transition. Select one, and we are given a preview. If it looks good, tap outside of the menu. The transition will be labeled by its name, as shown in the following screenshot:

12. For our final slide, we'll select the blank gradient and insert a chart using the plus icon in the upper-right corner of the screen, as seen in the next screenshot. Select a chart, and it will populate the center of the slide. We're able to manipulate the chart in the same manner that we did the image. This time, new options appear when you have the chart selected. **Edit Data** will allow you to edit each region in your chart. Tapping the brush icon while the chart is selected will give us options for editing the chart. Options such as **2D** and **3D**, as shown in the following screenshot, as well as options such as **Legends**, **Fonts**, and many others are available:

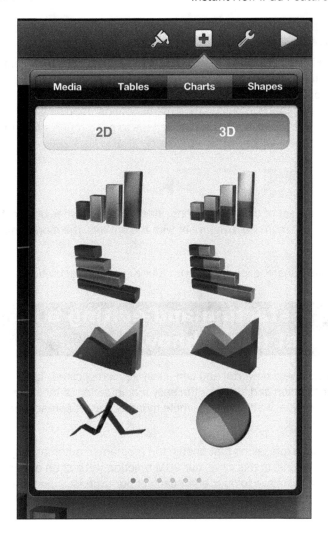

13. Now we have three slides. A title slide with an image and title text, a bulleted slide, and a slide with a chart. Tap the play button in the upper-right corner, and we've completed a brief presentation. Tap on each slide to play through our presentation, and if there's anything you'd like to change, it's as easy as tapping on the slide in the left-hand menu to edit it. The project is complete; you can tap **Presentations** in the upper-left corner of your presentation, and you'll be taken to the main **Keynote** menu.

How it works...

Using the plus sign is very important in Keynote. We used it to start a presentation and add an image, additional slides, transitions, and a chart. The plus sign is a running theme throughout the iWork suite. Tapping on objects is how we select the elements we want to edit. We tapped on images, slides, and graphs to pull up their menu options. Tapping is the most intuitive gesture on an iPad. Use the plus sign and utilize taps to get through a few more projects for practice.

There's more...

Each object contains a set of different options. Insert different types of objects and have fun manipulating them. The more we experiment with the options, the more familiar we'll become with the interface.

In the next recipe we'll share, export, and sync your Keynote presentation.

Numbers – starting and editing a spreadsheet (Must know)

Numbers, like Excel, is very powerful and can easily get complicated. Tap-and-drag gestures help ease the complication and allow for the easy manipulation of tables and easy creation of functions. In this recipe, we'll create a simple monthly budget spreadsheet using the SUM function.

Functions in Excel are expressions that enable the program to automatically perform mathematical calculations. In this case, our SUM function will add up our monthly expenses and give us a total. All we have to do is enter each of our expenses, and the function does the math for us, displaying the total in a specified cell.

Getting ready

Open **Numbers** and tap on the plus sign in the upper-left corner of the screen. Select **Create Spreadsheet**. We're going to select a blank sheet.

How to do it...

1. Start by selecting the **Blank** spreadsheet from the array of templates. Take a moment to look at the options. A lot of these templates are very useful and easy to utilize because all of the functions have been completed for us.

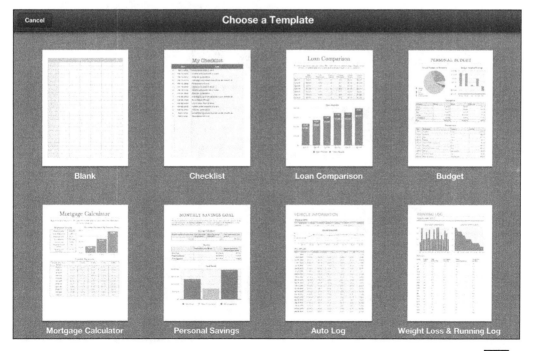

2. Our blank spreadsheet is pretty boring, so let's start formatting. Tap anywhere on the spreadsheet. We will see a vertical and horizontal bar with circles on each end. These circles adjust the number of rows and columns visible in a table. Use the pan gesture on each bar so that we have three columns and six rows.

3. While we're there, let's give it some color. Select the entire first row by tapping on the bar directly to the left of the first row. When it's selected, tap on the brush icon in the upper-left corner and select **Cells**. In that tab we'll see **Fill Color**. On tapping, a pop-up will appear with an array of colors. Choose a color for the top row. Below it, you'll see cells with a green fill.

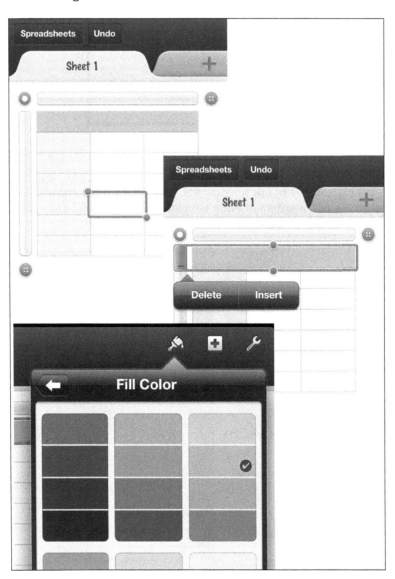

4. Now that it's got some color, let's get it looking and working like a monthly budget calculator. Begin by double-tapping in the first cell. The keyboard pops up and we're given four icons representing four inputs—numbers, date/time, text, and functions, as shown in the following screenshot:

5. Begin filling data in each row and column. Double-tap and select the input type. Once done, tap outside of the table. Label the contents of the spreadsheet as well as the data.

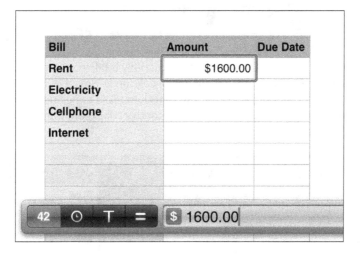

6. The keyboard will adjust itself depending on the input option we selected. In the preceding example, the number keypad was selected. In the following screenshot, we have the clock icon selected, so the keyboard is displaying in date/time:

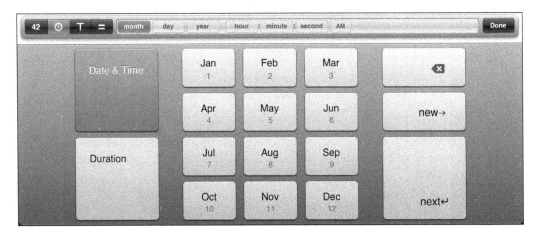

7. To finish up our budget and calculate our monthly total, we'll use the SUM function. Double-tap on a cell beneath the figures in column **B**. Select the equals-to icon so that the special keyboard pops up. Tap **functions**. This brings up a list of common functions. We want to calculate our total monthly bill expenditures, so select **SUM**, as shown in the following screenshot:

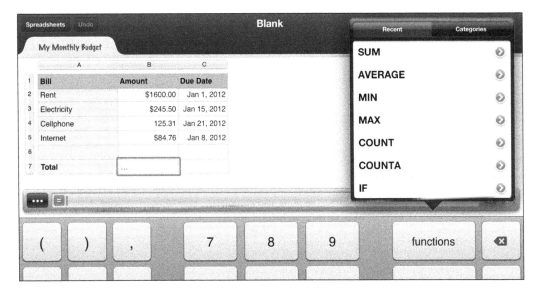

8. After selecting **SUM**, the input bar should reflect this by showing a SUM function. We're able to select the cells of which we want to add the values up by tapping and dragging the selection. Tap cell **B2** and drag the selection down to **B5**. We'll see the cells reflected in the input field. We can then save by either tapping outside of the table or selecting the green checkbox, as seen in the following screenshot. Are you getting the same total?

How it works...

It's just like Keynote, or any other app for that matter. A lot of tapping and double-tapping, using gesture intuitiveness, and familiar iconography allow you to create a spreadsheet quickly. That's all there is to it. You've created a basic spreadsheet using your iPad!

If you haven't done so already, you may want to rename the spreadsheet so that it does not display the generic name, **Blank**. Just as we renamed our presentation in the recipe on Keynote titled *Starting a Keynote presentation*, tap **Spreadsheets** in your budget document so that it takes you back to the main menu. Tap on the spreadsheet's generic title and rename it. In the next recipe, we'll be sharing this spreadsheet, so you'll want the name to represent what it is. Let's name it My Monthly Budget.

Functions are saved and viewable in Excel

Worried that all of your work, especially functions, won't be viewable in other applications? Well, all functions are usable in Excel and Open Office, so worry not! The same is true for when you import documents from those programs. Functions remain intact.

Pages – starting and editing a document (Should know)

Pages is the equivalent of Microsoft Word in iWork, and its touch interface makes it an entirely different experience. Editing involves a lot of tapping, twisting, panning, and dragging. In this recipe, we'll create a very basic document, inserting text, images, and shapes. We'll also discuss templates and just how useful they can be.

Getting ready

Open **Pages** and tap the plus icon in the upper-left corner of the screen, as shown in the following screenshot. Select **Create Document** and choose **Blank**:

How to do it...

1. Let's begin by creating a very basic document with some text, an image, and a shape. We'll be using the plus icon and its variations a lot as this is our way of adding elements to the page.

2. In our blank document, select the plus icon in the upper-right corner, as shown in the following screenshot:

3. Select a photo from the **Photo Library**. It will display on the page, and we're able to resize it by tapping and dragging on the circles surrounding the image. We can rotate our image by using the two-finger gesture, twisting the image around, as follows:

4. Let's go ahead and use the plus icon in the upper-right corner to select an arrow shape for our document, as follows:

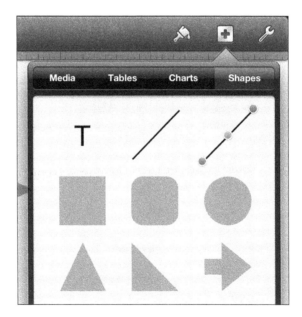

5. After you've selected the right-facing arrow and it's displaying on the page, tap and select **Copy**, duplicating the arrow so we have two arrows on the screen. Tap outside of the arrow and hit **Paste**. You can now position the arrows as you please.

6. Let's give **Copy** and **Paste** a try with the image we selected from our photo gallery. Tap to select the image, select **Copy**, tap outside of the image, and select **Paste**. We can always undo our work by tapping **Undo** in the upper-left corner. Tap and hold the **Undo** button and we see a **Redo** button appear. This will return our edit to its state prior to the undo action.

7. Now we've got two images and two arrows. Let's label our images with some text. Once again, select the plus icon in the upper-right corner of the screen. In **Shapes**, just as we did for the arrow, we'll select the **T** icon. A textbox appears, and the keyboard will pop up. Let's describe our images by adding text and moving it around the page. This will give us a final result of two images, two shapes, and two text fields, as shown in the following screenshot:

That's all there is to it. We've created a basic document using three elements.

How it works...

We use the plus icon a lot when we're creating documents from a blank page. Along with the plus icon, utilizing tools such as **Copy**, **Paste**, **Undo**, and the options within the brush icon will help with all of your element needs. Formatting text is a bit more complicated, and for that, it's best to start with a template. This helps us gain an understanding of how to format text.

There's more...

Creating a document from a blank page isn't our only option, so let's run through using a template.

1. Back out of our newly created document by hitting the **Documents** button.

2. Tap the plus icon and select **Create Document**.

3. The top of the screen will say **Choose a Template**, and that's exactly what we'll do.

4. Select **Modern Photo Letter**.

5. After the page has loaded, tap on each paragraph of the page. Notice the upper formatting bar. The font size, paragraph style, and other elements will change in order to reflect the item's formatting. Tapping on the brush icon will give you a deeper look at the formatting, more so than the top formatting toolbar. Inspect the images and notice the differences in the upper toolbar, such as font size and styling, as shown in the following screenshot:

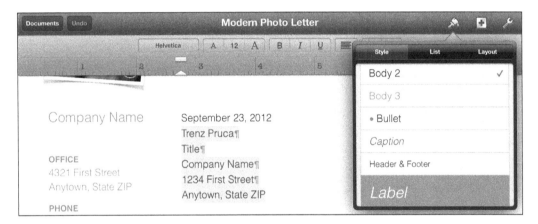

Have fun playing with the different templates. It's the best way to hone your formatting skills.

In the next recipe, we'll share the basic document we just created. We'll breeze through it as we find it to be almost identical to sharing in Keynote and Numbers.

Sharing and syncing documents from Keynote, Numbers, and Pages (Should know)

Sharing your presentations, spreadsheets, and documents is very similar across all of the apps in the iWork suite. In this recipe, we'll get into the basics of sharing in different formats for different applications.

All three apps, Keynote, Numbers, and Pages, can share documents as PDFs. Keynote can share a presentation as `.ppt` for use in PowerPoint. Numbers can share a spreadsheet as `.xls` for use in Excel. Pages can share a document as `.doc` for use in Word.

If the apps are installed on other OS X or iOS devices, documents will automatically sync to iCloud, provided iCloud is enabled and you are using the same Apple ID. Files are also available for viewing and download on `www.icloud.com`.

In the following recipe, we'll cover each method of sharing, using the document we created in the previous recipe.

Getting ready

Start on the home screen of **Pages**. If still in a template document, select **Documents** in the upper-left corner of the screen:

How to do it...

Once on the home screen of **Pages**, let's share using the **Edit** button.

1. Tap **Edit** in the upper-right corner of the screen.

2. Select the document we just created, and tap on the text to give the document a name. Once named, tap **Done** in the upper-right corner of the screen.

3. Tap on the document, and then on the share icon in the upper-left corner of the screen. You will see a list of options, as shown in the following screenshot:

4. You also have the option of sharing from within the document we created. To do this, tap to open the document.

5. Tap on the tool icon in the upper-right corner of the screen.

6. Select **Share and Print**. You'll see a list of options, as shown in the following screenshot:

7. E-mailing is a great way to share files for use within Microsoft Word, PowerPoint, and Excel. Selecting **Email Document** will give us three formats to choose from. We see the three formats in the following screenshot:

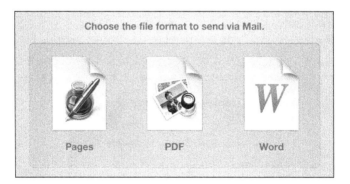

8. Selecting one of the options in the preceding screenshots will bring up an e-mail window containing the file in the body of the e-mail.

9. The second option under **Share and Print** is **Print**. It gives us the ability to wirelessly print our files by a printer sharing the same network. To check whether there's a printer on our network, we tap **Print**. This will list out any printers the iPad is able to print to, as shown in the following screenshot:

10. **Open in Another App** is a great way to share your files across many applications. There are many different apps that are able to read the formats that sharing enables us to use. This includes file formats such as .doc, .xls, .ppt, and .pdf. After tapping **Open in Another App**, tap the **PDF** file format and then tap **Choose App**. In the following screenshot we see examples of the different apps our .pdf file can be shared to:

11. **Copy to iTunes** is probably the least common way to share. Tap **Copy to iTunes** on the **Share and Print** menu. We're prompted to select the file format, and immediately after selecting, it saves the file so that we are able to access it when our iPad is plugged into our computer on iTunes.

   To access that presentation, we have to plug the iPad in to our computer. Once plugged in and open in iTunes on your desktop or laptop, select the iPad and click on the **Apps** tab on the top navigation bar of the screen. Scroll to the bottom; of the list view of applications, to the left, we see the apps that are capable of sharing documents with our computer. In the following screenshot, we see the document of **Numbers** we created in the recipe titled *Numbers – starting and editing a spreadsheet*. Here, we can click and save it to our computer, or we click and transfer it to our iPad.

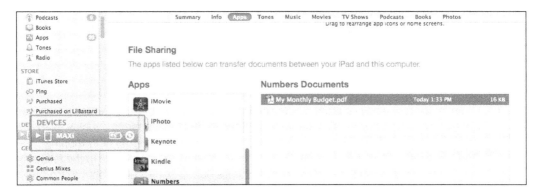

12. The **Copy to WebDAV** option is advanced and beyond the scope of this book. **Web Distributed Authoring and Versioning** (**WebDAV**) is a protocol; in other words, it is a standard for sharing and editing documents on a server.

There's more...

iWork is a perfect example of user interface ubiquity. Sharing is almost exactly the same in every app within the suite. Completing the sharing tasks here prepares you for sharing in other apps, all of which are synchronized to your devices, accessible via iCloud, and viewable by other popular programs.

In the following recipe, we'll cover iBooks, a great application that can be used in conjunction with files we share in iWork, the most common of which is the PDF.

iBooks – downloading from iBookstore and importing PDFs (Should know)

The best way to read books on the iPad is with iBooks. iBookstore carries a huge collection of books. Classics, such as Shakespeare's plays, and children's books, such as *The Ugly Duckling*, are available for free. Many books, especially those for children, offer amazing multimedia within the book itself, with the ability to tap on images for sounds or move them around the page.

iBooks is also a great application for reading PDF files. It renders the documents wonderfully and helps keep them organized and accessible for offline viewing.

In this recipe, we'll go over everything you need to know about using iBooks, from purchasing books and importing PDFs to organizing your collections.

iBooks does not come built-in to the new iPad, so let's open the **App Store** app and download it. Tap in the search box located in the upper-right corner of the screen and search for **iBooks**. The app is free, so tap on the **Free** button, and then tap **Install App**.

Now, let's open up the app and get started by downloading some books.

How to do it...

1. Let's begin by tapping **Store** in the upper-left corner of the screen, as seen in the following screenshot. This will take you to iBookstore, Apple's book version of the App Store. It looks and works in the exact same way as that of the App Store:

2. There are a lot of different ways to browse the store. We'll be looking for free books. In the lower navigation bar of the store, we see **Featured**, **NYTimes**, **Top Charts**, **Categories**, **Browse**, and **Purchased**. All are great ways to explore. For the sake of time, let's click on **Browse**, as shown in the following screenshot:

You'll get a list view in the left column with the default view being **TOP AUTHORS**.

3. Select **Free** from the upper-left corner, and you'll get a list of all free books sorted in the alphabetical order of the top authors. Select a free book by tapping on the **Free** button next to the book of your choice.

This will save it to our book library, where it's available for offline reading.

4. Let's try an alternative way of getting good free books. Go back into the store by tapping **Store** in the upper-left corner of the screen, as we did in an earlier step. In the lower navigation bar, tap **Top Charts**. We have hundreds of free books to browse through and download.

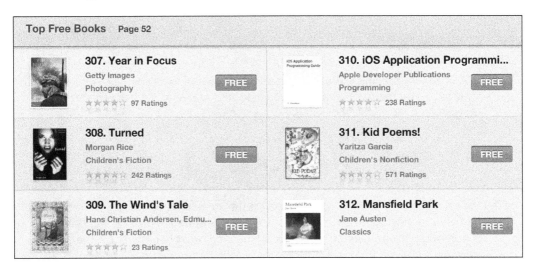

5. The ability of iBooks to import, display, and organize PDF files is one of its best features. To illustrate how easy it is, we'll download a PDF file from the web and import it into iBooks. Go to `http://www.reneevaldez.com/ibooks.pdf` in Safari, either by clicking on the link (if you're reading a digital version of this book) or by typing the URL into Safari manually.

6. When the PDF loads, we see **Open in "iBooks"** and **Open in...** in the upper-right corner within the browser window, as shown in the following screenshot:

7. Select **Open in "iBooks"**. That imports the document to our iBooks collection.

Importing is easy and can be done from many applications, e-mail and a web URL being the most common.

There's more

The following topics cover how books can be imported into iBooks via other applications and how we can organize our library:

Importing via other applications

To import via any other application, keep an eye out for an **Open in "iBooks"** button available in the share icon. See the following screenshot for an example:

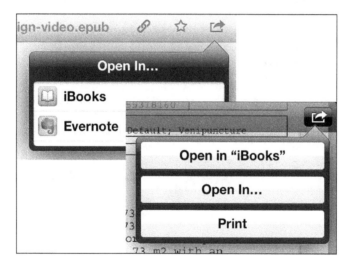

Organizing your library using Collections

With iBooks, organizing books is as easy as organizing apps. Tap **Collections**, and we can create a collection or view collections that we've already created. The following screenshot shows a list of collections with the **New** and **Edit** buttons:

To move books or PDF files into a category, we need to tap **Edit** in the upper-right corner of the screen. This changes the top menu so that we can select the items we wish to move into a category or delete. The following screenshot shows the **Move** and **Delete** buttons. We're now able to organize our library:

Garageband – a basic project (Become an expert)

Garageband is a powerful and robust music application capable of creating and recording music. It's basically a recording studio on the go. We'll go through setting up a basic project and then explore the features that make it a great app for your new iPad, even if you're a novice.

[This is a paid Apple application priced at $4.99.]

We'll begin by setting up a basic project and then dive a little deeper into some of its features.

Getting ready

Download Garageband from the App Store. The application is needed to complete the exercises in this recipe. Remember, it costs $4.99. We'll want to download over Wi-Fi to avoid consuming monthly data. The app file is large in size at around 800 MB. After the download is complete, open up Garageband.

How to do it...

1. Using the plus icon located in the upper-left corner of the screen, we'll select **New Song**.

2. Let's begin by recording a few bars of piano notes, so we can familiarize ourselves with the menu bar and all of the options at our disposal. We use the plus icon in the upper-left corner of Garageband's home screen.

3. We're immediately taken to a screen where we can select our instrument of choice. Selecting **Keyboard** brings up the keyboard with piano keys.

4. Let's go through the menu at the top of the screen, as shown in the screenshot after the following list:

   ❏ **My Songs** will take us back to Garageband's home screen.

   ❏ **Instruments** will pull up the swipeable menu of instruments (fun to play with).

   ❏ **Undo** (tap and hold for **Redo**) functions just as it does in all other applications.

   ❏ The piano keys icon will display our selected instrument. It will change depending on the instrument in use. So, if we were to be tracking drums, a drum icon would be displayed.

   ❏ The track icon displays the song's tracks that we've created.

   ❏ In the center of the menu are familiar playback controls with the inclusion of the record button, the one with the red center, that appears at the top, in the center of the screen.

   ❏ Next you have the volume bar. Slide to the left or right to adjust playback volume.

   ❏ The music note with the beam is an interesting icon, and one for advanced users. It's a collaboration button that allows you to start "jam sessions" with other iOS users on the same network.

   ❏ The sliders icon displays the instrument's effects. There are several options such as **Echo**, **Reverb**, and **Panning**.

   ❏ The tool icon contains our track settings.

   ❏ The question mark icon is the help menu.

5. Let's tap on the record button and play some notes on the piano keys. We see the top track indicator turn red as we record. Press the stop button.

6. Now the length of the track is displayed in green and we've recorded some notes, as shown in the following screenshot:

7. After we've recorded a few bars of piano notes, tap on the track icon located to the right of the piano keys icon in the top menu, as previously shown. This will allow us to edit our track.

8. Tap on the track so it turns green, and play with the length. Double-tap and you get a menu of options including copy, paste, and delete.

How it works...

In this recipe, we learned how to record some bars of music by selecting the piano and using the record button. This is step one in starting a project. Try repeating the process with other instruments. Using the track icon and the plus icon in the lower-left corner of the screen, you can add as many instruments as you want.

There's more...

Swiping through all of the available instruments and recording options shows how versatile the app is. For someone interested in recording using a real guitar, there are options for that as well! The following screenshot shows a sample of the components of a project:

In the preceding screenshot, there are some images of amplifiers. Using a gadget called iRig, we have the ability to record the guitar straight into Garageband while running the guitar signal through a multitude of amplifiers. Playing with all of the amps and pedals makes this one of its greatest features.

Sharing and syncing to iCloud

This is all very similar to sharing in other Apple applications.

Tap on **Edit** in the upper-right corner of the Garageband home screen, which displays all of the projects. Your songs will begin to shake. Select the song that we just created and note the icons in the upper menu, as shown in the following screenshot:

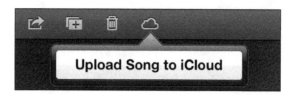

We have a share icon, a plus icon, a trashcan icon, and a cloud icon. Clicking on the cloud enables uploading your song to iCloud for editing on other OS X and iOS devices. The slightly modified plus icon is a duplication tool. It will copy the song you currently have selected.

Other ways to share include Facebook, YouTube, iTunes, and Mail.

This was a very brief overview because Garageband really deserves its own book. As one of Apple's applications optimized for the new iPad, it just had to be included in this book. It showcases the power of the new iPad quite well.

Thank you for buying
Instant New iPad Features in iOS 6 How-to

About Packt Publishing

Packt, pronounced 'packed', published its first book "*Mastering phpMyAdmin for Effective MySQL Management*" in April 2004 and subsequently continued to specialize in publishing highly focused books on specific technologies and solutions.

Our books and publications share the experiences of your fellow IT professionals in adapting and customizing today's systems, applications, and frameworks. Our solution based books give you the knowledge and power to customize the software and technologies you're using to get the job done. Packt books are more specific and less general than the IT books you have seen in the past. Our unique business model allows us to bring you more focused information, giving you more of what you need to know, and less of what you don't.

Packt is a modern, yet unique publishing company, which focuses on producing quality, cutting-edge books for communities of developers, administrators, and newbies alike. For more information, please visit our website: www.packtpub.com.

Writing for Packt

We welcome all inquiries from people who are interested in authoring. Book proposals should be sent to author@packtpub.com. If your book idea is still at an early stage and you would like to discuss it first before writing a formal book proposal, contact us; one of our commissioning editors will get in touch with you.

We're not just looking for published authors; if you have strong technical skills but no writing experience, our experienced editors can help you develop a writing career, or simply get some additional reward for your expertise.

PUBLISHING

Teaching with iPad How-To

ISBN: 978-1-84969-442-1   Paperback: 86 pages

Use your iPad creatively for everyday teaching tasks in schools and universities

1. Learn something new in an Instant! A short, fast, focused guide delivering immediate results.

2. Plan your lessons on iPad and share notes quickly.

3. Use exclusive iPad 3D resources for more engaging learning.

4. Use your iPad for creating and giving presentations.

Flash iOS Apps Cookbook

ISBN: 978-1-84969-138-3   Paperback: 420 pages

100 practical recipes for developing iOS apps with Flash Professional and Adobe AIR

1. Build your own apps, port existing projects, and learn the best practices for targeting iOS devices using Flash.

2. How to compile a native iOS app directly from Flash and deploy it to the iPhone, iPad, or iPod touch.

3. Full of practical recipes and step-by-step instructions for developing iOS apps with Flash Professional.

Please check **www.packtpub.com** for information on our titles